D1132814

Unintentional Humor™

Celebrating the Literal Mind™

Brent Anderson

Inspired By: Brent Anderson

Written By: Linda Gund Anderson

**Cartoons By: Alan J. Lewis
and Brett Bednorz**

ISBN: 978-0-9834509-6-2 (perfect bind)
ISBN: 978-0-9834509-4-8 (spiral bind)

Printed in the U.S.A.

Books may be purchased directly from the publisher.
Special pricing for educational purposes and fundraising use.

GP Gund Publishing
PO Box 853
Ventura, CA 93002
(805) 320-5101
BookSales@UnintentionalHumor.com

ABOUT UNINTENTIONAL HUMOR

Unintentional Humor™ books and products were originally created to improve awareness of the communication challenges that occur for many people on the Autism Spectrum.

After our first printing, we learned that our book has a much broader appeal. Unintentional Humor™ is helpful for the millions of people who have immigrated to the USA and are considered English-language learners. It is also an effective teaching tool for students in elementary, secondary and post secondary classrooms around the country.

Unintentional Humor™ is currently being developed into a variety of formats, including classroom curriculum and interactive learning tools.

Based on true stories and creative cartoons, Unintentional Humor™ is a unique, fun and refreshing resource for people of all ages.

<u>OUR STORY</u>

My son Brent was a difficult baby, to say the least. He was intolerant of loud noises, different textures and unfamiliar situations. My mother's intuition told me that something wasn't right. Doctors said he would outgrow it, some suggested that I was overreacting, but I knew that this was not just a phase. By the time Brent was $2\frac{1}{2}$, preschools wouldn't accept him, friends told me he didn't play well with their children and people questioned my parenting skills when he threw tantrums in public. I read dozens of child rearing books, but still had no insight into what I was dealing with. I grew more frustrated and frightened, hoping that I would find someone to shed light on my situation.

Luckily, a move to Boulder, CO in 1989 provided me access to the staff at the Developmental Disabilities Center. In one appointment, I learned that I was not a "bad mother", but rather my son's biggest advocate. They confirmed that Brent was in need of intensive therapy and support. I was happy Brent finally had the services that he needed and extremely grateful for the support that I would also receive. It was an additional 10 years until Brent was finally diagnosed with Autism; a rare diagnosis when he was born in 1986.

In 1990, Brent began working with speech therapist Andrea Mann. Her expertise taught me about Brent's struggles with communication and language. We discussed the need for a book to teach the meaning of common words and expressions. Although it has taken over 20 years to complete, **Unintentional Humor™** is the result.

Writing this book has transformed my relationship with Brent. We now have an open dialogue about how his mind interprets language. We discuss our differences and laugh at the disparities in our worlds. I have come to believe that I am the one with the skewed interpretation of language, not Brent. Even though he sees the words just as they are written, his misinterpretations often cause frustration. We hope that **Unintentional Humor™** will help improve communication for everyone, and provide some laughs along the way.

ABOUT US

Brent Anderson is the inspiration for this book. He worked closely with the artists to ensure that the graphics represent how he "saw" the words. Brent's willingness to share his challenges are an integral part of the book and help spread awareness about life with autism. He lives at the Training for Independent Living program in Ventura, California.

Linda Gund Anderson is an advocate for people with disabilities. Over the years she has worked to improve programs and raise funds for worthy organizations. Recently, she co-founded the Celebrate Autism foundation with her daughter. A portion of the proceeds from the sale of this book will be donated to their foundation.

ACKNOWLEDGMENTS

We want to thank the many people who have "unknowingly" contributed to our book. Brent's incredible teachers & therapists: Francess Reda, Chris Fukai, Lizzie Feeney, Mark Twarogowski, Amy Thompson, Mark Wood, Philippe Ernewein and the entire staff of Denver Academy. Dr. Patrick Bacon, Tracey Anderson, Diane Heidel, and Norma Joosten. The supportive staff of the Training for Independent Living program in Ventura, CA. Service coordinator, Larry Rice and the invaluable Tri-Counties Regional Center.

Special thanks to our cartoonists and designers Alan J. Lewis and Brett Bednorz, and special contributor Andrea Mann, M.A., CCC

All of our family and friends, who support and accept Brent and embrace his world of "**Unintentional Humor**".

Most importantly, Jenny Anderson, the best sister and daughter anyone could ever have. She is an incredible source of support and a contributor to this book.

OUR STORIES

LEANING TOWER OF PIZZA

Brent was excited that on our family trip to Europe we planned to see the
"Leaning Tower of Pizza."

He was disappointed when we got there and they didn't sell pizza.

After explaining that it is actually called the "Leaning Tower of Pisa" he said he still wanted to eat pizza.

11

STOP BUGGING ME

When Brent heard kids in class say
"Stop Bugging Me"
he looked around
for the bugs.

YOU'RE DRIVING ME UP THE WALL

COUCH POTATO

Brent spent the weekend with his friend Jordan.

He came home and asked why he called his brother a **"Couch Potato."**

BASEBALL BAT

Brent was worried that they played
baseball with real bats...

SCHOOL OF FISH

PLAYING MUSIC BY EAR

CAN OF WORMS

My friend Holly and I were talking about having the
neighborhood homeowners meeting at my house.
She reminded me of the issues at last year's meeting
and I said, **"Let's not open that can of worms."**

Brent shouted from the other room,
"Mom, that would be gross."

<u>DOG EARED PAGES</u>

Brent heard his Grandpa say that he gets upset when
people **DOG EAR** pages of his books ...
Brent picked up a book and said,
"Papa, I don't see any dog ears in here."

MONKEY BUSINESS

Brent asked me what kind of
businesses monkeys had.

IN A NUTSHELL

Brent didn't understand why people
use this saying.

He asked me, "How does someone get in a nutshell?"

<u>LET THE CAT OUT OF THE BAG</u>

I was planning a surprise
party for one of Jenny's friends.

Brent overheard me on the phone
making plans for the big day.
I reminded him that he wasn't
allowed to tell anyone
about the upcoming surprise.

Shortly after hearing me say to Jenny,
"We have to make sure that we don't
Let the Cat Out of the Bag,"
he got upset and asked,

"Mom, why would someone put their
cat in a bag?"

SEA HORSE

When we went on our first trip to the beach,
Brent really hoped we would find a
"Sea Horse."

He was very disappointed when we did not.

THE MONKEY BARS

Brent was afraid of the **"Monkey Bars"**
when he was in Elementary School.
Sadly, he never went on them because he
wasn't sure if he would to turn into a monkey.

SURFING THE WEB

IT'S RAINING CATS & DOGS

GOLF NUT

People say that
Uncle Jim is a
"GOLF NUT."

JELLYFISH

Brent knew that Jellyfish lived in the ocean,

but he thought that they made jelly.

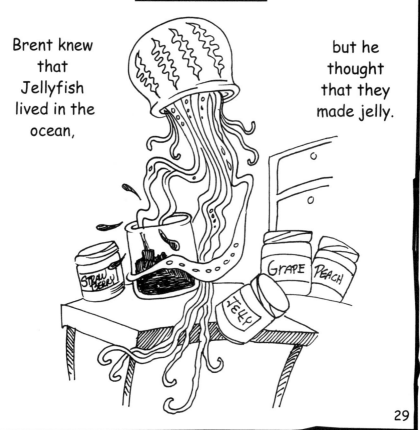

BANK HOLD UP

Brent heard about this on the news and asked me how anyone was strong enough to do that.

<u>FUNNY BONE</u>

Brent came into the kitchen
laughing and said to Jenny,
"I think I found my
"funny bone".

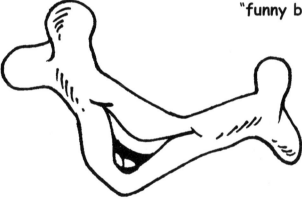

Jenny was excited and asked if he would
help her find her funny bone...

CARD SHARK

Brent learned on a family trip that Jason
is sometimes called a
"Card Shark"!!

BROKEN RECORDS

I usually have the news on when Brent and
I are eating breakfast in the morning.

One day he asked why the weather man was
talking about people "**Breaking Records**".

TURN INTO A PRUNE

Brent always loved to spend a lot of time
playing with his toys in the bathtub.

One night he announced that he did not
want to take baths anymore ...

When I asked him why he said,

"Because Grandma told me
that if I spend too much time in the bath,

I will turn into a Prune."

Very upset, he said,
"I don't want that to happen."

CHILL OUT

Brent didn't understand why people say this,
especially when it's not even warm outside.

HALF OFF

Brent was confused
by the signs
in toy stores that said:

50% OFF

He asked me,
"Why would someone want only
HALF of that toy?"

He was sure it wouldn't work any more
if it was broken in half.

<u>WHAT TIME?...WHAT DAY?...</u>

I called Brent to find out what date his summer school class was ending so I could make plans for our vacation.

The first question I asked was, "When does your class end?"

His response,
"It ends at 3 o'clock."

I took a deep breath and asked my second question.

"Can you please tell me what **DAY** your class ends."

His reply,
"It ends on Thursday."

OH, YOU WANT THE DATE...

I thought for a moment, then asked him
in the proper way,
"Brent, what is the **DATE**
that your ecology class ends?"

Quickly, he responded,
"July 23rd."

When I ask the question correctly, I always
get the response I am looking for...

CAR POOLS

<u>DUCK TAPE</u>

EAT LIKE A HORSE

After hearing his Uncle use the expression
"Eat Like a Horse"
Brent explained in great detail how the horses at
the Colorado Therapeutic Riding Center were fed.

YOU'RE IN THE DOG HOUSE

One day I found Brent
wandering around the back yard.
He was looking in the bushes and
around the area where our
dog usually sleeps.

I came outside and asked
him what he was doing.

He replied, "Looking for Dad."

I reminded him that
his Dad was at work.

Confused, he replied,
"You said he was in the
DOG HOUSE."

43

<u>COMPUTER MOUSE</u>

Brent came home after spending the day at Countryside Montessori School with Jenny.

I asked him what fun jobs he had done that day. He said he was really happy that they had worked on the computers.

He added, "except I could never find out where the **Computer Mouse** was."

ONLY A $5.00 BILL

I took Brent to the store to practice purchasing items on his own. I watched as he picked out a soft drink and a bag of chips and took them to the register. The clerk told him that his total was, "Two dollars and sixty five cents."

He looked at me and said, "Mom, I don't have that much. **I only have a $5.00 bill.**"

<u>GIVE ME A RING</u>

The kids and I were at the mall when I ran into my friend Mary. We talked for awhile and before we left I told her that she should, **"give me a ring"** in the next few days.

When we got in the car Brent asked,

"Why is Mary going to give you a **RING?"**

47

BRINGING HOME THE RAIN

Jenny had recently arrived home after
her first semester of college in
Tacoma, Washington.

The three of us had gone into a local bookstore
under sunny skies. As we were leaving
the store we were surprised by
an unexpected rainstorm.

Running to the car, Jenny said,
"I can't believe I brought the rain
with me from Washington."

After we had been home for about an hour,
Brent whispered to Jenny,

**"Jenny, did you really bring the rain
home with you?"**

49

FROG IN YOUR THROAT

Brent came home from school and shared, "My teacher said he was having a hard time talking in class, because he had a **frog in his throat.**"

"I looked at him all day, but I never saw the frog."

SPEAK UP IF YOU WANT TREATS

Brent was given clear instructions for watching our dog,
Jessie over the weekend. I left him notes telling
him when to feed her, walk her, etc.
I even bought a special box of dog biscuits
for him to give her while I was gone.

When I returned home,
I was upset to find
the box of dog biscuits
had not been opened.
I asked Brent why
he hadn't given
Jessie any
treats.

His response, "She didn't say she wanted any."

STARVING STUDENTS

A few years ago on Mother's Day,
I took my 19 year old daughter, Jenny,
and 21 year old son, Brent,
out to a nice dinner and a play.

As I pulled out my credit card to pay
the dinner bill, Jenny said,
"I'm sorry Mom, we should be buying
your dinner, since today is Mother's Day.
Unfortunately, we are
Starving College Students,
and we can't afford to."

Brent quickly chimed in,
"Jenny, I am not starving myself,
I've actually been gaining weight."

CLOUD NINE

After learning about my promotion at work,
I told Brent that I felt like I was on "**Cloud Nine**".

He went outside, looked up at the sky and asked,
"Which cloud is that, Mom?"

<u>DON'T LET THE BED BUGS BITE</u>

My kids stayed at home with a babysitter so that I could go to the movies with my friend, Kate.
When I got home, Brent was not in his bed. I found him asleep on the floor in my room.

I woke him up and asked him why he was sleeping on the floor.

He said, "I am afraid of the bugs."

I responded, "There aren't any bugs in your bed. What makes you think that?"

"Because the babysitter told me,

GOODNIGHT, SLEEP TIGHT, DON'T LET THE BED BUGS BITE."

I AM NOT A CHICKEN

Brent came home from school in tears. I sat him down and asked what had made him so upset.

Through his sobs, he explained that at recess he was afraid to go on the big slide, and some of the kids started calling him a chicken.

"Mom, I told them **I am not a chicken—I am a BOY!**"

PULLING MY LEG

One day Brent asked me,
"Why does Uncle Mac keep telling me he's
Pulling My Leg?"

FIRED FROM YOUR JOB

I picked up Brent from a friend's
house and he was very upset.
He said that he had overheard a phone
conversation that Matt's Mom
was having with
one of her friends.

He explained that she had been
crying when she learned
that her husband had been
fired from his job.

Brent asked me,
"Is Matt's Dad going to
get hurt when he is,

"Fired?"

HIT THE BIRDIE

Brent learned about the game Badminton and was very upset when he learned that you are supposed to hit the **"Birdie"**!!

FISHING TACKLE

Brent had learned about tackling from watching football. Trying to explain this was challenging.

<u>BRAINSTORM</u>

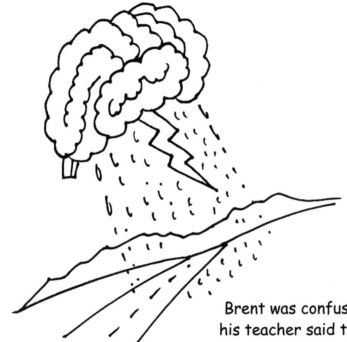

Brent was confused when his teacher said they were going to brainstorm ideas for school fundraisers.

<u>CONFUSING STREET SIGNS</u>

On a drive through Utah, Brent was excited when he saw this sign.

He said he didn't know that eagles lived on the highway.

EAGLES
ON
HWY.

Other confusing signs:

NO
STANDING
ANY
TIME

R ✕ R

SLOW
CHILDREN

DEAD
END

When Brent saw this sign on a trip to the mountains he said, "Why would someone want to stand on this road?"

PARKING RATES

Brent and I were picking up my friend Robin at the airport. We parked in the short term parking lot and went inside to meet her.
As we were leaving, he noticed that the sign at the payment booth said:

PARKING RATES:

$1.00 per ½ hour

$8.00   Maximum

After thinking about it for awhile, he asked,

"Where do you park if you need to stay at the airport for more than 4 hours?"

CATCHING RAYS

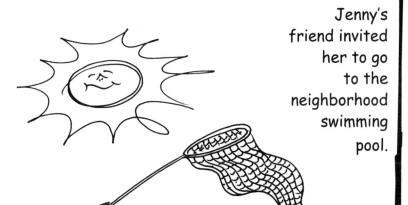

Jenny's friend invited her to go to the neighborhood swimming pool.

Brent called me at work to ask if I knew where our butterfly net was.
"Why?" I asked him.

"Jenny said that she and Melanie are going to **"Catch Rays."**

65

BACKSEAT DRIVER

When Jenny was taking her MasterDrive classes she became quite opinionated about my driving techniques. One day I told her she was acting like a **"Backseat Driver."**

Brent responded, "How can she do that Mom? She can't reach the pedals from back there."

THE TEACHER SAID SO

Brent was not always a popular kid in the classroom.
He became known as the 'Little Dictator'
because of how literally he interpreted the
teachers instructions to the class.

When the teacher would say, "Let's turn off our
computers and come back to our desks,"
Brent often took it upon himself to turn off
all the computers...
even when classmates were still using them.

When the art teacher would tell students to
put away their projects,
Brent sometimes took brushes
and paints out of other student's hands...

Even when he got into trouble because of this behavior,
his reply was always the same,
"The teacher said so..."

POT LUCK DINNER

I told Brent that we had been invited to a potluck dinner and I was having a hard time trying to decide what I was going to bring.

Later that evening he said, "I don't know what you're worried about Mom."

"Don't you take your **LUCKY POT** to the potluck dinner?"

WRONG SIDE OF THE BED

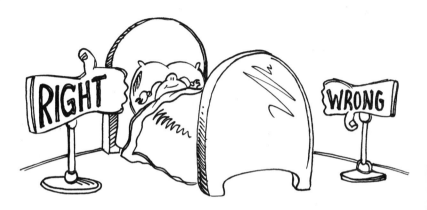

One morning during breakfast
Jenny was in a particularly bad mood.
I asked her if she had gotten up on the
"WRONG SIDE OF THE BED".

Brent quickly ran upstairs to his room
and shouted down,
"Mom, how do I know if I got up on the
Right or the **Wrong** side of the bed?"

CAT GOT YOUR TONGUE?

When Brent spends the entire day
with his Grandparents, it often includes
going out to eat with their friends.

During one of their outings, they
encountered my father's retired business
associate. Trying to engage Brent in the
conversation, Mr. Simpson asked him
what school he attended.

Brent hesitated a bit before he
came up with the answer.

My Dad then said,
"What's the matter,
Cat Got Your Tongue?"

Brent said, "What cat?"

PIG OUT

ELBOW GREASE

A good friend came over to help with some home
improvement projects at my house and
I asked if Brent could be his helper.

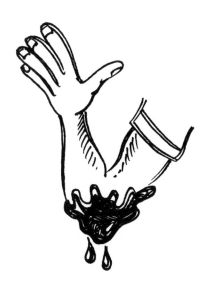

Encouraging him to work
a little bit harder,
he suggested that
Brent needed to use more
Elbow Grease.

Brent asked,
"Uncle Mike, where do
I get some of that
Elbow Grease
that you are using?"

UNDER THE WEATHER

I had plans to meet my friend Tracy for dinner.
Around 4:00, I received a call
from her husband telling me that she wasn't
feeling well and needed to cancel.

Brent overheard me say,
"Nathan, please tell Tracy I am sorry that she is
"Under the Weather".

When I got off the phone I saw
Brent looking curiously out the window.

He asked me, "Why did you say that
Tracy is under the weather?"

"It is sunny outside..."

I GOT STOOD UP

Brent saw Jenny on her bed crying
and asked her what was the matter.

"Henry **stood me up**," she said.
Brent replied,
"Then why are you lying down?"

<u>GIVING AWAY THE BRIDE</u>

Our family was watching a T.V. program
that featured a large celebrity wedding
that was being held in our hometown.

The announcer was providing descriptions of
the church, the flowers, the bride's dress,
and the families of the bride and groom.
She gave details of the wedding party while showing
video of the bride walking down the aisle.

After the announcer commented,
"the **Bride was given away by her Father**"

Brent, who was watching the show
with me said,

"THAT'S MEAN"...

LET'S HAVE T.V. DINNERS

My Mom picked up Brent and Jenny
to take them to dinner and
then sleep over at her house.

When they got to the restaurant,
they found out the kitchen was experiencing
problems and was not able to serve customers.

Knowing the kids were hungry and that she didn't
have anything ready to eat at her house,
she suggested that they go to the
grocery store and pick up T.V. dinners.

Brent was surprised and told his grandmother,
"Namie, I've never eaten a
T.V. for dinner before."

BROKEN HEART

My sister and I went to lunch at the mall. She was very upset about the recent breakup with her boyfriend. She told story after story of their difficulties and how many times he had broken her heart.

Later, at home, Brent asked me, "When is Aunt Beth going to the hospital to **fix her broken heart?**"

YOU LOST A TOOTH

One evening at dinner Jenny announced that earlier in the day she had, **"lost a tooth."**

Brent quickly jumped up from the table and ran into the play room. I watched him as he began pulling toys out of the toy box.

I said, "Brent, what are you doing?"

His response, "Looking for Jenny's lost tooth."

FAVORITE TEAMS

Because of Brent's love of wildlife, he only
liked sports teams with animal names.
He envisioned them looking like this:

"THE BEARS"

"THE BULLS"

<u>Some of Brent's other favorite teams:</u>

Colorado Buffaloes   Anaheim Mighty Ducks
Miami Dolphins   Washington Huskies
San Jose Sharks   Arizona Diamondbacks

<u>NO CRYING OVER SPILLED MILK</u>

Jenny came home from school very upset.
She told me that there had been a
fight at lunchtime between
some of her friends.

I told her that while things seemed
difficult right now, she shouldn't worry.
In a day or two the girls would
forgive each other and it wouldn't
seem important anymore.

I must have used the expression,
"There is no use crying over spilled milk,"
because Brent ran into the kitchen and asked,

"WHO SPILLED THE MILK?"

CLOSE THE WINDOW

I got home from work and found the windows open during a pouring rainstorm.

When I walked in the family room Brent was watching T.V., unaware of the rain coming in the house.

Angrily, I said, "I told you to close the windows if it started raining."

He said, "You did, Mom, but **you didn't tell me which ones!!**"

CUT A RUG

One day Brent asked me what the expression, **"Cut A Rug"** means.

He laughed after I explained it to him.

A few weeks later, when I was getting ready
to go to a party he said,
"Don't forget to take your scissors, Mom."
I asked him, "Why?"

He snickered and said,
"So you can **cut a rug**!!"

3 STRIKES AND YOU'RE OUT

With close friends involved in
Major League Baseball, Brent has been
fortunate to attend many
Colorado Rockies baseball games.

Over the years, I had explained the rules
to him, and I assumed that he had a
good understanding of the game.

When we started working on this book,
he shared how he always felt sorry
for the baseball players that were
"thrown out."

I never realized that he thought the players
had to leave the game and go home.

TIME FLIES WHEN HAVING FUN

My kids spent the day with my good friend, Meg. After a few hours she looked at her watch and commented, "I can't believe that it's almost time take you home. I guess it's true that

"Time Flies When You're Having Fun".

Brent heard her say this, looked around, and said, "Where? I don't see it."

<u>WILD GOOSE CHASE</u>

I took the kids to the mall to find some items my
friend Liz wanted for her birthday.

We went from store to store, asking if anyone
knew who sold the items we needed.
We received a lot of different answers,
but never found what we were looking for.

After four hours, I told the kids
that I felt like we had been sent on a
"Wild Goose Chase"
through the mall.

Brent had a puzzled look on his face and said,
"I didn't see any geese at the mall today,
did you Jenny?"

91

<u>200,000 MILES</u>

I decided to purchase a conversion van that Brent and I could travel in. After spending a great deal of time researching used vans, I made a list of 6 that I wanted to test drive. Knowing that Brent would be spending a lot of time in the van, I took him with me to L.A. for a day of "car shopping".

On our drive, I asked Brent to read the information I had gathered on the first van we were going to see.

"It is a 1997 Dodge with 200,000 miles," (long pause) . . . "that's really good," he said. I asked him why that was good and he replied, "Because that's how many more miles it has to go."

After a long conversation, Brent learned that the number of miles on a car odometer are how many miles ALREADY traveled, not how many they have left to drive!!

HAPPY CAMPER

STORIES SHARED BY OTHERS

PIECE OF CAKE

After one student called their spelling test a
"PIECE OF CAKE,"

other classmates began complaining,
   "I didn't get a piece of cake."

STOP THE HORSEPLAY

A boy asked his mother, "What does Daddy mean when he tells us to, **stop that horseplay?**"

DRESS THE TURKEY

While discussing what recipes we should make for Thanksgiving dinner, my Grandmother asked me what I liked to use to dress the turkey.

My son said,

"Grammy, why would you want to **Dress The Turkey?**"

<u>ALL EARS</u>

A Mom shared that she was working in her
daughter's 3rd grade classroom on a day
they were having a guest speaker.

The teacher told the kids that
they needed to be
"ALL EARS"
during the presentation.

She saw her daughter raise her
her hand and ask the teacher,

"Where do I get some more ears?"

<u>RECYCLED CHRISTMAS TREES</u>

A few days
after Christmas,
my husband and I were
discussing which one
of us was going
to take our Christmas
tree to the
Recycling Center.

Our son thought for
awhile and then said,

"I wonder if we will
get the same tree
again next year..."

FINGER FOODS

A mom came home from work exhausted and told
her kids she was too tired to make dinner.

"Let's just have **finger foods** tonight," she suggested.
Horrified, her daughter shouted,
"Mom, why would you make us do that?"

POOR TEACHER

On the last day of school, my son was
saying good-bye to his 4th grade teacher.

I listened while he told her about our
summer plans. At the end of their conversation,
I was surprised to hear him say that
when he grows up he is
planning on giving her money.

When we got to the car I asked him,
"Why did you tell Mrs. Johnson that
you are going to give her money?"

"Because I heard you tell
Grandma that she is a
"Poor Teacher."

HIT THE SACK

My kids were having a sleep over at our neighbors.

After watching TV and playing games until 10:00, Sharon came in to tell them it was time to **"Hit the Sack."**

My son asked his sister, "Why does she want us to do that?"

THE LOCKER ROOM

My daughter loved to swim.
It was a favorite activity of hers until
I took her to the local recreation center
to use their new indoor pool.

The pool rules required everyone to
shower before getting in the water.
I told my daughter that we had to go
into the locker room to rinse
off before we could go swimming.

She started crying and said,
"Mom, I don't want to go in the

LOCK HER ROOM..."

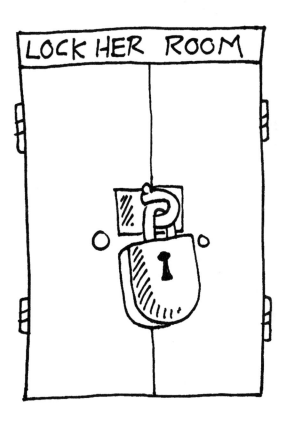

FARMER IN THE DELL

AIRPLANE HANGARS

<u>CAT FISH</u>

While at a Seafood Restaurant, my daughter saw
that they had
catfish on the menu.

I heard her giggle and whisper, "MEOW..."

<u>GROSS NATIONAL PRODUCT</u>

A father shared his story of
dinner table conversation
he recently had with his daughter.

"My daughter and I talked about
how confused she was
by a topic they had discussed
in her High School Economics class-

the "**Gross National Product.**"

She asked me,
"Is that because all of
the products are gross?"

<u>CHICKEN WITH ITS HEAD CUT OFF</u>

My son went to stay with our friends in
San Diego for the weekend.
It was a big deal because he was going
to visit all by himself.

He called home one night because he was
confused about something that had
been said during dinner that evening.

"Lynn said she was running around like a
chicken with its head cut off
when she was at work today."

My son asked me,
"Why would she say that, Mom?"

LAME DUCK

A teacher shared the story of a student who came into her office very confused by what he had heard in History class.

"We learned that after a certain amount of time, our President becomes a **"Lame Duck"**.

Confused, he asked me, "Why would the President turn himself into a duck?"

WE'LL BE THERE WITH BELLS ON

My sister called to tell me she was finally
marrying her long time boyfriend.
"We'll be there with bells on..." I told her.

Later that week, my daughter and I went shopping
for outfits to wear to the wedding.

She asked, "Mom, when do we get the bells
we're going to wear?"

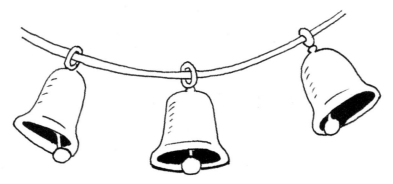

THE FUNNY FARM

My son was watching a T.V. show and a character commented that their neighbors needed to go to the **"Funny Farm"**.

He asked me if I thought our neighbors should go to the Funny Farm.

My answer required a lot of explaining.

<u>OUR FOUR FATHERS</u>

My nephew was staying at our house and I was helping him with his homework.
We were discussing the constitution and how it had been written by the Forefathers of our Country.

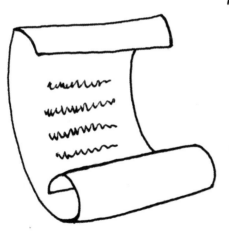

My son must have been listening to our conversation, because at bedtime he said,

"I can remember Jefferson, Lincoln and Adams, but who was the fourth of the **FOUR FATHERS?**"

117

ROAD CLOSED

We loaded the entire family into the car for a weekend trip to the mountains.

About an hour outside of town my husband said, "The weather is so bad, I'm afraid they may close the road."

My son asked, "Mom, how do they set up the doors?"

BULL IN A CHINA CLOSET

I HATE CHANGE

My daughter overheard my friend Colleen telling me,
"I don't like change."

Thinking she knew a good solution, she said to her,
"Why don't you use your credit card?"

GRANDPARENT STORIES

Stories shared after spending time
with their Grandparents.

"Grandma always knows
what we are doing
because she has eyes in
the back of her head."

"Grandma and
Grandpa lived when
they didn't even have
television.
What do you think
they did all the
time?"

"Did you know that
Grandma had to walk
Uphill Both Ways
to go to school?

BEAN
HILL

"Grandpa said
that things
today don't
amount to a
"Hill of Beans"?

THAT GIRL IS HOT

My brother called to tell me about the humorous situation that occurred while he was at a restaurant with my son. He commented that the waitress was "**Hot**" and my son replied,

"It is hot in here, why doesn't she do something to cool down?"

<u>DOWN IN THE DUMPS</u>

We were doing projects around the house.
My friend Bill asked my son to ride along
with him to take some items to the local dump.

My son asked,
"Is that where people go who are really
Down in the Dumps?"

KEEP YOUR EYE ON THE BALL

A Mom was playing catch with her son and said to him,

"Remember to keep your **"eye on the ball."**

When she threw the ball back to him, he immediately put the ball over his eye.

Trying not to laugh, she realized that he did exactly what she told him to do.

SANTA CLAWS

A mom shared her sadness after learning why her son
was so scared of having his picture
taken at the mall with
"Santa Claws".

APPLE OF MY EYE

BREAK A LEG

At the school play someone told my daughter to

"break a leg."

My son replied, "I hope she doesn't, Mom."

YOUR STORIES

Write your experiences of Unintentional Humor:

_____
_____
_____
_____
_____
_____
_____
_____
_____
_____
_____
_____
_____
_____
_____
_____
_____
_____
_____
_____
_____
_____
_____
_____

YOU CAN SHARE YOUR STORIES WITH OTHERS
ON OUR WEBSITE:
www.UnintentionalHumor.com

GLOSSARY

GLOSSARY

DEFINITIONS

FUNNY BONE: This is not actually a bone, but a point on your elbow where the ulnar nerve runs over the humerus bone. (Humerus sounds like humorous = funny) When you hit this spot it gives a very weird, tingling sensation, and it is not funny at all.

PLAYING MUSIC BY EAR: This describes someone that can play music after listening to it, without looking at any notes. Some people also say that you are "Playing it by Ear," if you are doing something that is unplanned.

COUCH POTATO: This describes someone that leads a very inactive lifestyle. This is usually a person who spends a lot of time on the couch watching television.

145

KEEP YOUR EYE ON THE BALL: This is a way of telling someone to stay alert and pay close attention to what is happening around them. It may be said when you are playing a sport and need to catch or hit a ball.

CUT A RUG: This is a slang expression for dancing. It originates from the idea that you may have to move rugs out of the way to dance or can describe someone who dances so much that they wear a hole in the rug.

STOP BUGGING ME: This is said when someone is bothering you. It comes from the word, "pester." Bugs are also known as pests, which is where this expression gets its meaning.

<u>BULL IN A CHINA CLOSET:</u> This describes a person that is causing trouble or breaking things. China is fragile dishware and a strong bull would cause a lot of damage if allowed near it. It can also mean aggressiveness or pushiness.

<u>YOU ARE IN THE DOG HOUSE:</u> This is said about a person that is in trouble or someone is very angry with. If a dog has misbehaved, they may be forced to stay in their dog house, which is most likely a punishment.

<u>BROKEN RECORDS:</u> A way to recognize higher levels of achievement than have not been met before. It can be used in reference to sports records and weather temperatures, among other things.

<u>RAINING CATS & DOGS</u>: A heavy downpour. One theory on this saying, is that the Norse god of storms was pictured with dogs and witches supposedly flew with their cats during the rain. Thus, a rainstorm is symbolized by cats and dogs.

<u>SURFING THE WEB:</u> Someone that is on the internet-formally known as the World Wide Web (www.) and commonly called "the web". Surfing is the verb that describes searching through channels or networks for information, not riding waves.

<u>MONKEY BUSINESS</u>: This describes someone that is being mischievous, annoying and not behaving properly. It can also be said about someone that is clowning around or being disrespectful.

A FROG IN YOUR THROAT: This describes a person with a hoarse or croaky sounding voice. Long ago, Medieval physicians placed frogs into patients throats believing that their secretions could cure a cough. Good thing they realized that was wrong.

ALL EARS: This is said when someone is expected to listen closely, not to miss a thing. When using this expression, the speaker wants people to pay attention, focus on nothing else and listen intently.

BROKEN HEART: A way to describe someone that is very sad. It implies great emotional pain and may be used when a relationship ends or when a person very close to you dies.

YOU'RE PULLING MY LEG: A way to refer to someone that is teasing you or playing a joke on you. It could also be said about a person that you think is lying to you.

CHILL OUT: People use this expression to tell someone that they should calm down and not be upset. It may be said to a person that is very scared or nervous about something.

HIT THE SACK: This is common saying for someone that is going to bed. It originated long ago when people slept on sacks of hay, before they had mattresses. People sometimes say, "hit the hay", which means the same thing.

CAT'S GOT YOUR TONGUE: This describes someone that is having a hard time thinking of what to say or is not able to answer a question quickly. Some people may think your silence is suspicious.

NO CRYING OVER SPILLED MILK: This means that you should not get upset over things that are not important or have already happened, because usually there is nothing you can do to change them.

THE FUNNY FARM: This is a slang term used for a mental institution or a place where people go when they are having mental problems. Sometimes these people are considered, "funny in the head".

IN A NUT SHELL: This is said if you are describing something in a very brief or concise way. If you don't want to hear all of the details of a story you might say, "just tell me in a nutshell."

HAPPY CAMPER: An informal way to describe someone that is very happy or satisfied. It could also be used to describe a person who is unhappy, by saying; "not a happy camper".

T.V. DINNER: Frozen pre-made meals that come in serving trays that can be easily warmed and eaten off of your lap or on a small table. Many people eat these while watching television.

<u>HOLD UP A BANK:</u> The definition of a "hold up" is a delay, or informally it means an attempt to rob (or steal) from someone with a weapon. It is common to refer to a bank robbery as a "bank hold up".

<u>DON'T LET THE BED BUGS BITE:</u> This saying is part of a popular nursery rhyme & poem that has been said to children before going to sleep for years. Although, there are real bed bugs that can live in mattresses, you probably don't have them.

<u>CAR POOLS:</u> In this term the word pool means grouping together resources for a common advantage. People who share rides in the same car save fuel and money and help the environment by emitting less gas pollutants.

153

JELLYFISH: Jellyfish are one of the oldest living creatures, with over 350 known species, occupying every ocean on the planet. It is NOT where jelly is made and they are actually not even a fish.

OPEN A CAN OF WORMS: This is a way of saying that you may create new problems while trying to solve others. It is often used to warn of complicated matters by saying; "don't open that can of worms."

YOU STOOD ME UP: This describes a person who you have made plans with that doesn't show up, leaving you alone waiting for them, and usually very angry.

<u>TURN INTO A PRUNE</u>: After spending a long time in water, people's fingers and toes swell and become very wrinkly, sometimes looking similar to a prune. A prune is actually a dried plum.

<u>PIECE OF CAKE</u>: This is a common way to refer to something that is considered very easy. The saying originated during World War II by British soldiers who said the expression, "easy as pie," which means the same thing.

<u>TIME FLIES WHEN YOU'RE HAVING FUN</u>: This expression is often said when you feel that time is passing quickly while you are enjoying yourself.

155

THE WRONG SIDE OF THE BED:
This may be said about someone that is having a very bad day. Most commonly said in the morning, especially if a person wakes up in a bad mood.

WILD GOOSE CHASE:
This saying is used if you feel you have wasted time searching for something that cannot be found. It was used by Shakespeare to describe following someone on an erratic course.

HORSEPLAY:
This describes rough play, fooling around, fake wrestling or many different types of "kids play". Based on the knowledge that young horses like to frolic, run and charge to release energy. It also may be called, "Horsing Around".

LET THE CAT OUT OF THE BAG:
The expression was used to describe a dishonest merchant promising a pig but selling a cat. Most people use it to refer to someone who reveals a secret without meaning to.

FOREFATHERS: The confusion with this is the word 'FORE', which sounds like the number four (4). A Forefather is a member of a past generation who contributed to a common cause. Much of our history came from our Forefathers.

FINGER FOODS: Food that is eaten directly from your hands, rather than food eaten with a fork, knife, spoon or other utensil. Examples of finger foods are; pizza, fried chicken, french fries and hamburgers.

<u>ELBOW GREASE:</u> This describes working very hard, especially doing manual labor. It is not an oil or cream that can be used to achieve positive results, but rather the hard work and effort you must put in for great accomplishments.

<u>BACKSEAT DRIVER:</u> Someone who is a passenger in a car that insists on telling the driver how to operate the vehicle, even though they are not the one who is driving.

<u>DUCK TAPE:</u> Also known as "Duct Tape". It is very strong, flexible tape with a cloth backing. It is usually gray or black in color and is commonly used by the military. It is water resistant and has many uses.

POTLUCK DINNER: A gathering of people where each person or group of people contributes a dish of food to be shared among the group. This is common way for people to have a party.

GOLF NUT: People are often referred to as a "nut" when they are extremely devoted to a particular interest. It can be used in many different ways; motorcycle nut, history nut & sports nut are examples.

CLOUD NINE: This is a common way of describing great happiness. It comes from the weather bureaus rating of clouds. A large cloud is rated a nine (9) when it reaches over 40,000 feet.

159

PIG OUT: This describes someone that has eaten way too much food. Sometimes people like the food so much that they eat more than they should and actually make themselves sick.

LAME DUCK: This refers to an elected official who is still in office but has not been re-elected. In the U.S.A., the President can only serve two terms and is often called a Lame Duck in the 2nd term.

DOG EARED PAGES OF A BOOK: The folded down corners of book pages, which is often done to mark your place. It also can be said when describing a worn out or overused book.

THAT GIRL IS HOT: This is a slang term said about someone who is very attractive and enjoyable to look at. It can be used for both men and women. It is not the same as hot which describes the temperature.

AIRPLANE HANGARS: A hangar is a closed structure that protects airplanes and spacecraft. It is spelled differently from hangers which is what you use to hang your clothing on.

CATCHING RAYS: A narrow beam of light is known as a ray. Sunlight is often called rays. People who are suntanning or spending time in the sun often say that they are "catching rays".

161

<u>CAT FISH</u>: This is a group of ray-finned fish that come in many shapes and sizes. They all have distinctive barbels by their mouth, which look like the whiskers on a cat.

<u>RECYCLE YOUR TREE</u>: In recent years, it has become common for people to recycle their Christmas trees. The trees are put through a machine that grinds them and turns them into garden mulch. They are not used as trees again.

<u>HIT THE BIRDIE</u>: In the game of badminton, the shuttlecock is often referred to as the "Birdie" because it is made out of real feathers. In competition, it has 16 feathers, which usually come from the left wing of a goose.

COMPUTER MOUSE: A hand held device that controls the cursor on a computer screen. It is called a mouse because some people think it looks like one with a small body and the cord as the tail.

DOWN IN THE DUMPS: This saying has been used for hundreds of years to describe feelings of sadness or depression. The dump is also a place where large amounts of trash are taken. They are not the same.

YOU'RE A CHICKEN: This is a common way to describe someone that is afraid or scared. Chickens are considered cowardly animals because they usually run away when people approach them.

163

CARD SHARK: Someone who is very skilled at playing cards is often called a "card shark". Since they often win, people may think they are cheating. A person good at billiards may be called a, "pool shark".

YOU'RE DRIVING ME UP THE WALL: This is said when someone is really bothering or annoying you. You may feel like climbing the walls to escape them. A person may also say, "You're driving me crazy," which means something very similar.

THE MONKEY BARS: Playground equipment is sometimes referred to as "monkey bars", because of the many ways children can climb and swing on them. This is similar to what monkeys do in the wild. It may also be called a "Jungle Gym".

<u>UNDER THE WEATHER</u>: This describes a person who is sick or not feeling well. Because some people believe that bad weather can make you sick, people use this term to describe someone who is ill.

<u>SCHOOL OF FISH</u>: A group of fish are called a "school". Fish swim together in schools as protection from predators, and to more easily find food. (They also are smarter when they are in school!!)

<u>FISHING TACKLE</u>: All of the gear that is used for fishing is called the tackle. Items such as hooks, lures, weights and line are often kept in a container called a "Tackle Box".

165

APPLE OF MY EYE: This is a common expression used to describe someone that you cherish above all others. It was used by Shakespeare and can also be found in passages in the Bible.

BRAINSTORM: This refers to a group of people who work together to come up with solutions for issues or problems. It is believed that more people sharing ideas is better than someone working alone.

BREAK A LEG: This is a common way to wish "good luck" to an actor or performer before they go on stage. Some people believe that by saying the opposite of what you really want you will prevent something bad from happening.

FIRED FROM YOUR JOB:
Americans often use the term "getting fired" when they are asked to leave their employment. This term implies that it is the employees fault, unlike someone leaving a job willingly.

DRESS THE TURKEY:
Made up of bread crumbs and seasonings, this can be cooked inside or outside of the turkey. It is called both "stuffing" and "dressing", but it is usually the same.

SEA HORSE:
A seahorse is a species of marine fish in a group called "hippocampus". "Hippo" comes from the Greek word meaning horse and "kampos" means sea monster. The mythical "sea-horse" is shown as part horse and part fish.

167

CONTACT US

CONTACT INFORMATION

We are currently at work
on our next book.
If you are interested in
sharing your stories and
having them included in
Unintentional Humor™
    Volume 2
send them by email to:

VOLUME

                   UnintentionalHumor@gmail.com

or through our website:

               www.UnintentionalHumor.com

Please connect with us on:

facebook

**Unintentional Humor™
Book fan page**

@Unintentl_Humor

CELEBRATE AUTISM

As our book title suggests, we prefer to "**celebrate**" our differences and believe that by increasing awareness of language disparities we can improve understanding and acceptance.

The Celebrate Autism Foundation has been created to fund organizations that support and encourage the gifts of autism. If you want to receive more information about our organization, please email us:

CelebrateAutism@gmail.com

If you would like to have Brent & Linda share their **Unintentional Humor**™ presentation with your group or organization please contact:

Linda Gund Anderson

805-320-5101

lindagundanderson@gmail.com

__ABOUT AUTISM__

Autism is the fastest growing serious developmental disability in the U.S.A. In 2006, the CDC estimated diagnosis of 1 in 110 children and 1 in 70 boys with its prevalence continuing to rise at astounding rates.   A new study published in the May, 2011 <u>American Journal of Psychiatry</u>, found rates as high as 1 in 38 children.

Autism is defined as a range of neurological and psychological conditions known as Autism Spectrum Disorders (ASD). The spectrum ranges from mild to severe, providing a wide variety of symptoms and challenges. Collectively, ASD has common characteristics which often include;
impaired social interaction, difficulty reading social cues and a literal interpretation of language.

We hope that **Unintentional Humor™** improves awareness, understanding and acceptance of the families and individuals living with Autism.